Contents

T0386071

Welcome

1 **Write. Then match.**

1 Hello. My name's Lindy.

2 _____. I'm Pippin.

3 _____. I'm Joe.

4 _____. My name's Princess Emily.

a

b

c

d

2 **Read and match.**

1 Hello! My name's Ann. What's your name?

2 My name's Mia. How are you?

a I'm fine, thank you.

b My name's Sam.

3 **Find and colour. Then write.**

1 = red	2 = yellow	3 = purple
4 = blue	5 = pink	6 = green

My name's _____ .

  4 **Read and write.**

What's your favourite colour? My favourite colour is _____ .

5 **Find and write.**

yaMdon _____   Fayrid _____

daTsuey _____   taSrayud _____

deWsenyad _____   dunSay _____

hurTdyas _____

 6 **Complete. Then read and say.**

What day is it today?

It's _____. It's _____!

_____ for _____.

4

Lesson 3 vocabulary (*What is it today? It's Monday.*)

Write and circle.

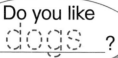 dogs   rabbits   snakes   parrots

1 Do you like dogs ? / Yes, I do. / No, I don't.

2 Do you like _____ ? / Yes, I do. / No, I don't.

3 Do you like _____ ? / Yes, I do. / No, I don't.

4 Do you like _____ ? / Yes, I do. / No, I don't.

8 **Read and write.**

Yes, I do.   No, I don't.

1 Do you like parrots? _____

2 Do you like fruit? _____

3 Do you like vegetables? _____

4 Do you like Mondays? _____

9  **Find and circle the words.**

e	n	m	j	u	n	e	d	l
b	o	a	p	r	i	l	e	j
a	v	y	l	g	e	o	c	a
u	e	j	u	l	y	c	e	n
g	m	a	r	c	h	t	m	u
u	b	c	s	j	l	o	b	a
s	e	p	t	e	m	b	e	r
t	r	h	p	b	d	e	r	y
f	e	b	r	u	a	r	y	a

10 **Follow and write.**

1 8

My birthday is in ⌁October⌁. I'm _____.

2 4

My birthday is in _____. I'm _____.

3 7

My birthday is in _____. I'm _____.

a

July						
1	2	3	4	5	6	7
8	9	10	11	12	13	14
15	16	17	18	19	20	21
22	23	24	25	26	27	28
29	30	31				

b

October						
1	2	3	4	5	6	7
8	9	10	11	12	13	14
15	16	17	18	19	20	21
22	23	24	25	26	27	28
29	30	31				

c

January						
1	2	3	4	5	6	7
8	9	10	11	12	13	14
15	16	17	18	19	20	21
22	23	24	25	26	27	28
29	30	31				

11 🔘 1:13 **Read and match.**
Then listen and check.

1 What's your name?

2 How old are you?

3 When's your birthday?

4 What's your favourite colour?

5 Do you like dogs?

6 What day is it today?

7 How are you today?

a It's in August.

b I'm fine, thank you!

c My name's Lindy.

d Blue.

e It's Tuesday.

f I'm eight.

g Yes, I do.

12 **Ask a friend and answer.**

1 What's your name?

2 What day is it today?

3 How are you today?

1 My toys

1 Look and write.

ball bike boat car doll kite teddy bear train

1

2

3

4

5

6

7

8

a It's a

_____.

b It's a

_____.

c It's a

ball

_____.

d It's a

_____.

e It's a

_____.

f It's a

_____.

g It's a

_____.

h It's a

_____.

2 **Look, read and circle.**

1  (**What's**) / What are) this?

It's a (ball / **doll** / teddy bear).

2  (What's / What are) that?

It's a (boat / bike / train).

3  (What's / What are) these?

They're (kite / kites / boats).

4  (What's / What are) those?

They're (bikes / bike / ball).

3 **Listen and write. Then draw and colour.**

1

It's a _train_.

It's _____.

2

They're _____.

They're _____.

3

It's a _____.

It's _____.

Lesson 2 grammar (*What's this / that? It's a car.*)

9

4 **Read and match.**

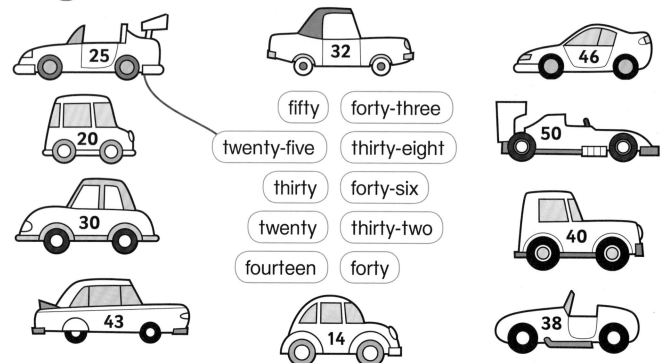

fifty   forty-three

twenty-five   thirty-eight

thirty   forty-six

twenty   thirty-two

fourteen   forty

 **5** **Look and match. Then write.**

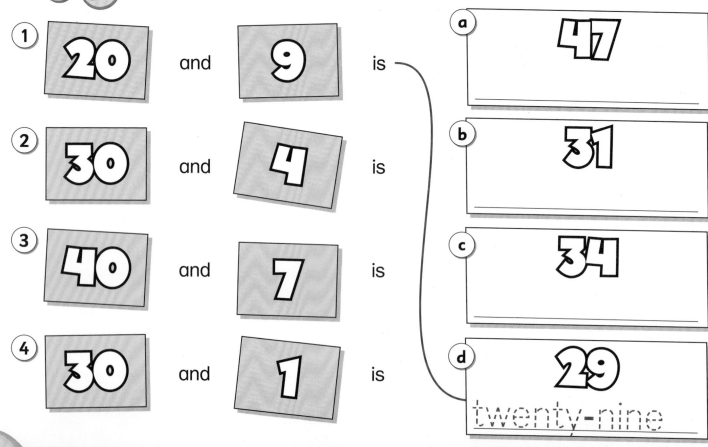

1   20 and 9 is

2   30 and 4 is

3   40 and 7 is

4   30 and 1 is

a   47

b   31

c   34

d   29   twenty-nine

6   **Look, count and write.**

1 How many ~~bikes~~ are there?

There are ~~fifteen bikes~~.

2 _____ are there?

There are _____.

3 _____ are there?

There are _____.

4 _____ are there?

There are _____.

7 Look and circle.

1 (Lindy / Princess Emily) is my friend.

2 (Lindy / Joe) is my friend.

3 (Lindy / Pippin) is my friend.

4 (Joe / Lindy) is my friend.

8 Look and tick (✓).
Then write about yourself.

1 a b

2 a b

Good friends play together and share toys.

Good friends listen and help.

Who is your best friend?

_____ is my best friend.

What do you like?

We like _____

and _____ .

9 Read the words. Circle the pictures.

ch   sh

fish   rich   shell   ship

10 1:26 Listen and link the letters.

| ch | c | h | sh |

START   p   f   b   FINISH

s   sh   ch   s

11 1:27 Listen and write the words.

1 ch i n   2 _ _ _ _   3 _ _ _ _   4 _ _ _ _

12 1:28 Read aloud. Then listen and check.

I can see a fish. I can see a shell.

13 **Look and write. Then find and draw the missing word.**

| car | boat | ~~helicopter~~ | bike | train | plane | lorry | bus |

1

1 h e l i c o p t e r

2

3

4

5

6

7

8

2

3

4

5

6

7

8

14 **Look through your window. Count and write.**

cars ☐   bikes ☐   buses ☐   motorbikes ☐

lorries ☐   trains ☐   planes ☐   helicopters ☐

Wider World

  Complete the picture and match.

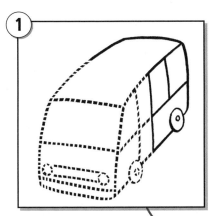

1

2

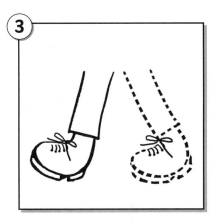

3

a I walk to school.

b I go to school by bus.

c I go to school by car.

  How do you go to school? Ask ten friends and tick (✓).

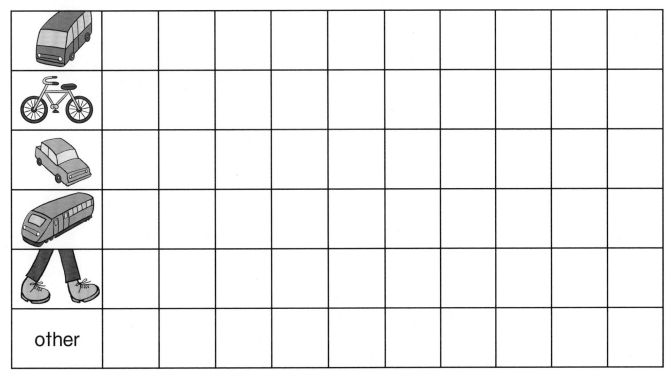

Unit Review

 17 Read and circle. Then colour.

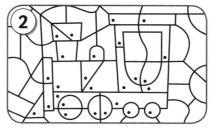

It's a (car)/ boat).
It's blue.

It's a (bike / train).
It's yellow.

It's a (doll / teddy bear).
It's purple.

 18 Look and circle. Then write.

1

(What's this?)/ What are those?

It's a ___boat___ .

2

What's this? / What are these?

They're _____ .

3

What's that? / What are these?

_____

4

What's that? / What are those?

_____

 19 Look at Activity 18. Count and write.

1 How many cars are there? There are _____ cars.

2 How many balls are there? _____

About Me

20 **Read and write. Then colour.**

teddy   bike   school   ~~favourite~~

These are my
¹ favourite _____ toys.

This is my favourite
² _____ bear. His
name's Fred and he's brown.

And this is my ³ _____.
It's red and black. I go to
⁴ _____ by bike.

21  **Draw your favourite toys and write.**

These are my favourite toys.

_____

_____

_____

_____

_____

2 My family

1 **Look and write.**

aunt   cousin   daughter   grandad   granny   son   ~~uncle~~

This is my dad.

This is my mum.

This is my brother.

This is my cousin.

1 This is my *uncle* .

2 This is my _____.

3 This is my _____.

4 This is my _____.

5 This is my _____.

6 This is my _____.

7 This is my _____.

2 **Look, circle, and write.**

~~aunt~~   cousin   uncle   daughter

1 Who's (he / (she))?

(He's / (She's)) my
aunt .

2 Who's (he / she)?

(He's / She's) my
_____ .

3 Who's (he / she)?

(He's / She's) my
_____ .

4 Who's (he / she)?

(He's / She's) my
_____ .

Look, read and write.

attic hall flat bedroom living room kitchen

Where's my granny?

She's in the <u>attic</u>.

Where's my uncle?

He's in the _____.

Where's my aunt?

_____ in the _____.

Where's my daughter?

_____ in the _____.

Where's my son?

_____ in the _____.

Where's my cousin?

_____ in the _____.

4   **Read and colour.**

1 There's a red car on the bed.

2 There's a purple car behind the backpack.

3 There's a blue car under the chair.

4 There's a yellow car on the desk. It's next to the lamp.

5 There's a green car in the backpack.

5 **Look at the picture again. Write *True* or *False*.**

1 There are two beds. _____

2 There are three desks. _____

3 There are six cars. _____

4 There's a lamp on the desk. _____

6 **Read and number.**

a

b

1   This is my mum.

2   This is my grandad.

3   This is my sister.

4   This is my dad.

5   This is my brother.

c

d

e

7 **Read and circle.**

1   Is Princess Emily happy?   Yes, she is. / (No, she isn't.)

2   Where are her mum and dad?   They're in the (castle / garden).

3   Where are her grandparents?   They're in the (castle / garden).

8 **Read and write. Then draw your relatives**

How many aunts have you got?

I've got _____.

How many uncles have you got?

_____

How many cousins have you got?

_____

9 **Read the words. Circle the pictures.**

~~bath~~   thick   thin   this

10 **Listen and link the letters.**

| s | th | th | th |

START   a   r   s   FINISH

th   z   ch   th

11 **Listen and write the words.**

1 This 2 _____ 3 _____ 4 _____

12 **Read aloud. Then listen and check.**

This is a thick book. That is a thin book.

13 **Listen and number. Then write.**

baby   grandparents   ~~parents~~   children

a

_____

b

_____

c

[1]

𝖕𝖆𝖗𝖊𝖓𝖙𝖘

d

[   ]

_____

14 **Read and match.**

They're young.   She's young.   They're old.   He's young.

Wider World

15 **Look and write.**

| boy | twins | girl |

1

I'm a _____ .

2

I'm a _____ .

3

We're _____ .

16 (1:50) **A treehouse home! Listen and number.**

Unit Review

17  **Read and write. Then match.**

1 Where's my daughter?

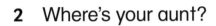
She's _____ in the garden.

2 Where's your aunt?

_____ in the house.

3 _____ my cousin?

He's in the flat.

18 **Read and draw.**

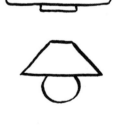

This is my bedroom. There's a TV on the table.
There are two teddies under the bed. There's a lamp on the chair!

About Me

19 **Read and write.**

| two | ~~aunt~~ | these | twins | garden |

This is my uncle and
¹ _aunt_ and
² _____ are my cousins.

They are in my ³ _____.

I've got ⁴ _____
cousins. They are babies.

And they are ⁵ _____.

20  **Draw some of your relatives. Then write.**

This is my _____

and _____.

_____

_____

_____

3 Move your body

1 **Look and write.**

| clap | move | nod | point | ~~shake~~ | stamp | touch | wave |

1

Shake your body.

2

_____ your arms.

3

_____ your head.

4

_____ your toes.

5

_____ your feet.

6

_____ your fingers.

7

_____ your hands.

8

_____ your legs.

Read and circle.

①

(He / **She**) can shake (his / **her**) body.

②

I (can / can't) touch (my / your) toes.

③

(He / She) can stamp (his / her) feet.

④

I (can / can't) wave (my / your) arms.

  Listen and number.

a

b

c

d

1

Look and match.

①

_____ ___ the splits

②

c ___ tch a b ___ ll

③

clim ___

④

thr ___ ___ ___ a b ___ ll

⑤

stand on your h ___ ___ ___ d

⑥

swi n g ___ ___

⑦

do cartwh ___ ___ ___ ls

⑧

swi ___

5 Look, write and circle.

| climb | do cartwheels | ~~do the splits~~ | swim |

1 Can he _do the splits_ ?

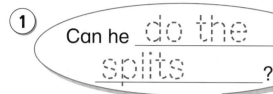

Yes, he can. / No, he can't.

2 Can you _____?

Yes, I can. / No, I can't.

3 Can he _____ _____?

Yes, he can. / No, he can't.

4 Can you _____?

Yes, I can. / No, I can't.

Lesson 4 grammar (*Can you jump? Yes, I can. / No, I can't.*)

31

6 **Read. Then circle the speaker.**

1 Jump! Shake your body!

2 Jump! Jump!

3 Hello! My name's Frank.

4 Exercise is good for you.

5 Clap your hands! Stamp your feet! Touch your toes!

7 **Write (✓) exercise or (✗) not exercise.**

1  ✓

2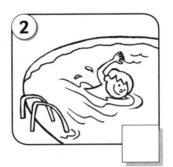

3

4

5

6

7

8

8 **Read the words. Circle the pictures.**

ng   nk

ink   ~~ring~~   sing   sink

9 (1:66) **Listen and link the letters.**

START —— g   nk   ng   c

n   sh   th   FINISH

ng   k   m   nk

10 (1:67) **Listen and write the words.**

1 p i n g   2 _ _ _ _ _   3 _ _ _ _ _   4 _ _ _ _ _

11 (1:68) **Read aloud. Then listen and check.**

Dad can sing. The girl can sing.

12 **Look and write.**

pull	
~~kick~~	
push	
skip	

1 kick

 13 **Read and find. Then number.**

Wave your arms.

Jump.

Clap your hands.

Touch your toes.

Skip.

Hop.

Wider World

14 **Look and write.**

| ballet dancer   athlete   basketball players   ~~footballer~~   gymnast |

1

2

3

She's a footballer.   He's a _____.   She's a _____.

4

5

He's an _____.   They're _____.

15 **Read and answer.**

| Yes, I can.   No, I can't. |

1 Can you run fast? _____

2 Can you kick a ball? _____

3 Can you touch your toes? _____

4 Can you point your toes? _____

5 Can you throw a ball? _____

Unit Review

16 **Look and write.**

| climb | do the splits | hop | skip | swim | swing |

She can ___climb___ . He can't _____ . _____

_____ _____ _____

17 **What can you do? Read and circle.**

1 I (can / can't) do cartwheels.

2 I (can / can't) swim.

3 I (can / can't) stand on my head.

4 I (can / can't) hop.

5 I (can / can't) do the splits.

6 I (can / can't) run fast.

7 I (can / can't) catch a ball.

8 I (can / can't) climb trees.

About Me

18 **Look and read. Then write *can* or *can't*.**

I ¹_____ dance
and I ²_____
skip. I ³_____
catch a ball and I
⁴_____ do cartwheels.

I ⁵_____ hop.
And I ⁶_____
touch my toes!

19  **Look and (✓) or (✗). Then write about yourself or a friend.**

I can _____

and I _____.

_____

_____

_____

4 My face

1 Look and write.

ears   eyes   ~~face~~   hair   mouth   nose

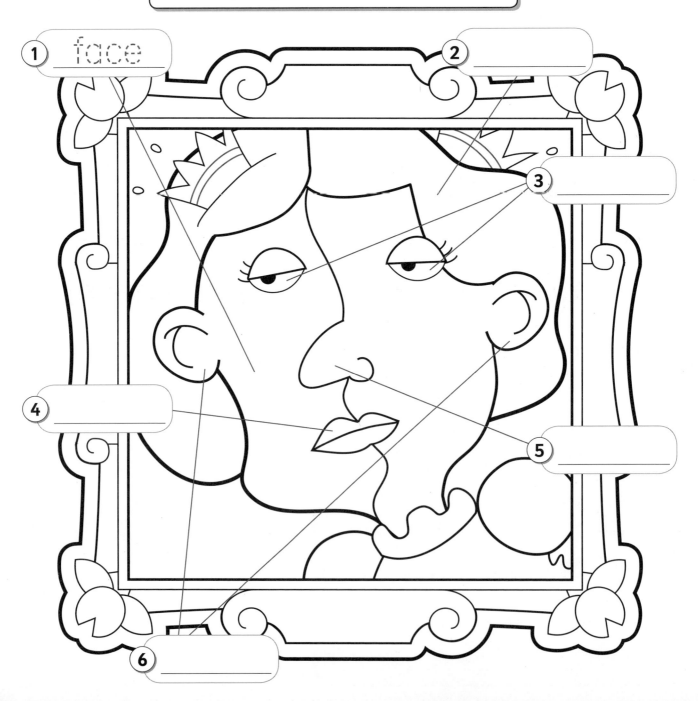

1 _face_

2 _____

3 _____

4 _____

5 _____

6 _____

2 **Read. Then look and write _1_ or _2_.**

a I've got big eyes. `2`

b I've got short hair.

c I haven't got a big mouth.

d I've got long hair.

e I've got small eyes.

f I haven't got a big nose.

3 **Look, read and circle.**

1 Have you got small ears?

Yes, I have. / No, I haven't.

2 Have you got long hair?

Yes, I have. / No, I haven't.

3 Has she got big eyes?

Yes, she has. / No, she hasn't.

4 Has he got a small nose?

Yes, he has. / No, he hasn't.

4 **Read and circle.**

1

She's got
((long) / short) hair.

2

She's got
(neat / messy) hair.

3

He's got
(long / short) hair.

4

She's got
(neat / messy) hair.

5

He's got
(blond / dark) hair.

6

He's got
(straight / curly) hair.

5 2:08 **Listen and tick (✓). Then draw.**

 ✓ big eyes  ☐ small eyes

 ☐ big nose ☐ small nose

☐ short, curly hair ☐ long, straight hair

6 **Listen and circle. Then look and write.**

Granny   Ruth   Max   Uncle Ed

1 (straight) / curly / (messy) / blond   It's _____Ruth_____.

2 messy / neat / blond / red   It's _____.

3 long / short / straight / curly   It's _____.

4 messy / neat / curly / dark   It's _____.

7 **Look at Activity 6 and write.**

1 Granny's hair is _____short and curly_____.

  Granny has got _____short, curly hair_____.

2 Ruth's hair is _____ and _____.

  Ruth has got _____, _____ hair.

3 Max's hair is _____ and _____.

  Max has got _____, _____ hair.

4 Uncle Ed's hair is _____ and _____.

  Uncle Ed has got _____, _____ hair.

5 My hair is _____ and _____.

  I've got _____, _____ hair.

Lesson 4 grammar (*My hair is curly.*)

Read and circle. Then colour.

1 Pippin's eyes are (big / small).

2 Pippin's head is (big / small).

3 Pippin's mouth is (big / small).

4 Pippin's nose is (big / small).

5 Pippin is (yellow and green / red and blue).

6 Pippin is (Lindy's / Princess Emily's) friend.

 Listen and number.

a

b

c

1

d

10 Read the words. Circle the pictures.

snail rain tail wait feet

11 2:16 Listen and link the letters.

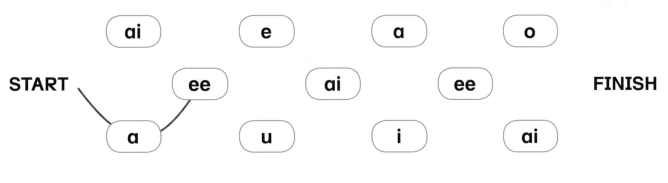

| ai | | e | | a | | o |

START   ee   ai   ee   FINISH

a   u   i   ai

12 2:17 Listen and write the words.

1 s ee   2 _____   3 _____   4 _____

13 2:18 Read aloud. Then listen and check.

The cat has got a tail. The cat has got four feet.

 **14** Count and write.

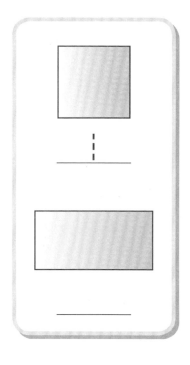

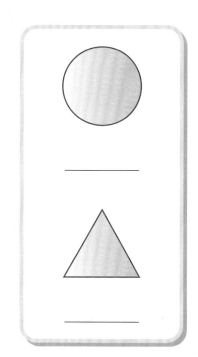

15 2:20 **Listen, look at Activity 14 and circle.**

1 (Yes) / No   **2** Yes / No   **3** Yes / No   **4** Yes / No

16 Draw. Use the shapes in Activity 14. Then write.

It's a _____.

Wider World

17 **Read and circle.**

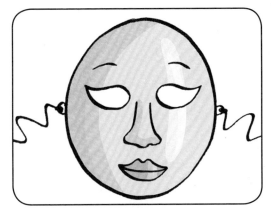

It's a (painting / mask).
It's a (man / woman).

It's a (mosaic / statue).
It's a (man / woman).

18 **Look at the mosaic pictures. Then write.**

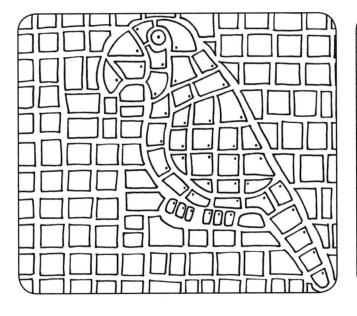

What's this?

It's a _____.

What are these?

_____.

Unit Review

19 **Read and write.**

1 Has she got big eyes?

_____Yes, she has_____ .

2 Has she got dark hair?

_____ .

3 Has she got small ears?

_____ .

4 Has she got a big nose?

_____ .

20 **Draw. Then read and write.**

1 He's got short blond hair. It's curly. Who is it?   It's _____ .

2 She's got long blond hair. It's straight and messy.

Who is it?   _____

3 She's got long blond hair. It's curly and neat.

Who is it?   _____

About Me

21   **Read and circle.**

me   George

This is me and my best friend.
[1](His / Her) name's George.

My hair is short and
[2](dark / blond). I've got
[3](big / small) eyes. My eyes
are brown. I've got a
[4](big / small) mouth and
[5](big / small) ears!

George's hair is [6](long / short)
and [7](dark / blond). His hair is
[8](neat / messy). He's got
[9](big / small) eyes and a
[10](big / small) mouth.

22 **Draw yourself and a friend and write.**

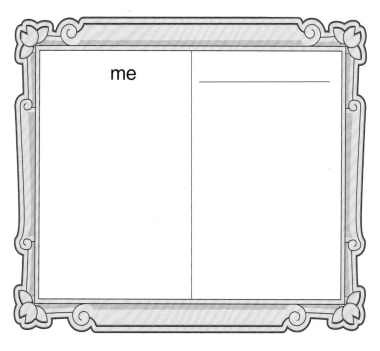

me

This is me and my best friend.

5 Animals

cow   duck   ~~goat~~   hen   horse   sheep   turkey

1. goat
2.
3.
4.
5.
6.
7.

2 (2:29) **Listen and number.**

a

b

c

d

3 **Look at Activity 2. Read, write and colour.**

1   What are these? They've got fat bodies and black feet. They're white. They've got black faces. They're _____ .

2   What's this? It's got a big mouth and two big feet. It's yellow. It's a _____ .

3   What's this? It's got a thin body and four legs. It's brown. It's a _____ .

4   What are these? They're big and black. They've got long tails. They're _____ .

Lesson 2 grammar (*It's got big eyes. It's black and white.*)

49

4   **Look and write.**

| frog | ~~bat~~ | skunk | owl | crow | rat | lizard | fox |

1 bat

2 _____

3 _____

4 _____

5 _____

6 _____

7 _____

8 _____

5 **Read, match, and write.**

1 It's got a long tail.
It's brown.

a

They're _____.

2 They're small and green.
They've got big eyes.

b

It's a _____.

3 They're thin and black.
They've got two legs.

c

They're _____.

6 **Read and circle the mistakes. Then write.**

1

It's a frog. It's (big.)

It isn't ___big___. It's ___small___.

2

They're goats. They're thin.

They aren't _____. They're

_____.

3

It's a duck. It's big.

It isn't a _____. It's a _____.

4

They're skunks. They're thin.

They aren't _____. They're

_____.

7 **Look at Activity 6 and write the answers.**

Yes, it is.   ~~No, it isn't.~~   Yes, they are.   No, they aren't.

1 Is the hen small? ___No, it isn't._____

2 Are the foxes thin? _____

3 Is the frog small? _____

4 Are the skunks thin? _____

Lesson 4 grammar (*It isn't big. It's small.*)

51

8 Match. Then circle the animal in the story.

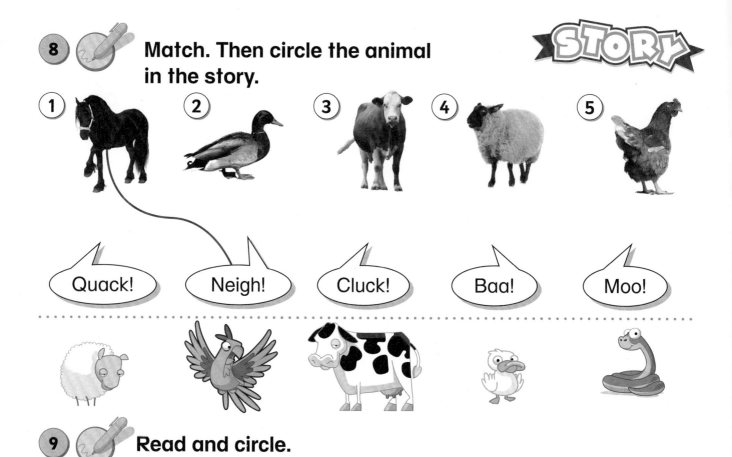

Quack! Neigh! Cluck! Baa! Moo!

9 Read and circle.

Pippin is a (duck / (parrot)) He is (red / brown) and (blue / purple). He ('s / hasn't) got wings. He's got (two / four) legs.

10 Look and match.

11 **Read the words. Circle the pictures.**

boat   goat   light   soap

12 (2:37) **Listen and link the letters.**

| a | igh | o | a |

START ———— i   oa   FINISH

oa   ch   i   igh

13 (2:38) **Listen and write the words.**

1 s igh ___   2 ___ ___ ___   3 ___ ___ ___   4 ___ ___ ___

14 (2:39) **Read aloud. Then listen and check.**

The goat has got some soap. The goat has got a boat.

15 **Look and read. Then write and circle.**

1

I'm a ___fox___.
I'm ((asleep) / awake) in the day.

2

I'm a _____.
I'm (asleep / awake) at night.

3

I'm an _____.
I'm (asleep / awake) at night.

4

I'm a _____.
I'm (asleep / awake) in the day.

5

I'm a _____.
I'm (asleep / awake) in the day.

| bat |
| cow |
| duck |
| ~~fox~~ |
| owl |

16 **Draw the animals from Activity 15.**

1

day

2

night

Wider World

17 **Look and match.**

1
a hen

2
an ostrich

a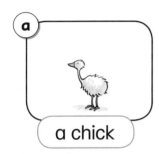
a chick

b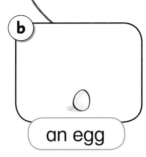
an egg

c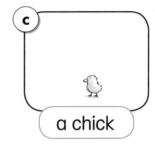
a chick

d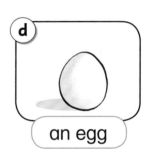
an egg

18 **Read and write *True* or *False*.**

1 Ostriches are birds. _____True_____

2 They aren't big. They're small. _____

3 They've got two legs. _____

4 They've got short legs. _____

5 They've got feathers. _____

6 The father ostrich is brown. _____

7 Ostrich eggs aren't small. They're big. _____

19 **Correct the false sentences.**

Ostriches are big. They aren't small.

_____

_____

Unit Review

20 (2:43) **Listen, tick (✓) and colour.**

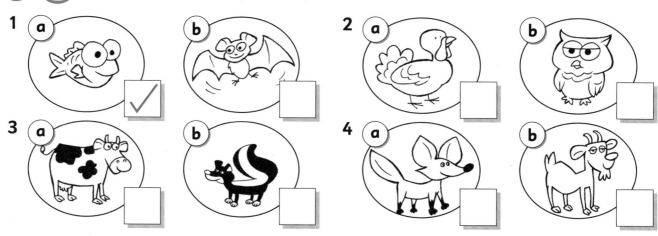

1 a b ✓

2 a b

3 a b

4 a b

21 **Look, read, and write.**

1 Is the cow big?

   Yes, it is.

2 Are the sheep white?

   _____

3 Is it a hen?

   _____

   It's an _____.

4 Are they foxes?

   _____

   They're _____.

About Me

22 **Read and write.**

fox   asleep   ~~white~~   awake   horse   big   four   tail

My favourite animal is big and

¹ white _____ .

It's got ² _____ legs and a

long ³ _____ .

It's got a ⁴ _____ nose.

It's ⁵ _____ in the day.

It's ⁶ _____ at night.

Is it a ⁷ _____ ?

No, it isn't. It's a ⁸ _____ !

23  **Draw your favourite animal. Then circle and write.**

My favourite animal is (big / small)

and _____ .

It's got _____

_____

_____

_____

_____

_____

6 Food

1 Look and write. Then draw.

1	eggs	✔
2	_____	✘
3	_____	✘
4	_____	✘
5	_____	✔
6	_____	✔
7	_____	✔
8	_____	✘
9	_____	✘
10	_____	✘

apples   fish
bananas   hot dogs
burgers   pizza
chicken   rice
eggs   salad

2 **Look and write.**

| hot dogs   bananas   ~~chicken~~   eggs |

1 I like _chicken_.

2 I don't like _____.

3 He likes _____.

4 She doesn't like _____.

 3 **Look at Activity 2. Read and match.**

1 Does Princess Emily like eggs?

2 Does Lindy like chicken?

3 Does Joe like bananas?

4 Does Pippin like hot dogs?

a Yes, he does.

b No, he doesn't.

c Yes, she does.

d No, she doesn't.

4 **Read and answer.**

1 Do you like burgers? _____

2 Do you like salad? _____

Look and match.

1

2

3

4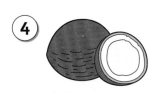

grapes	beans
toast	sweetcorn
potatoes	pasta
coconut	pineapple
pancakes	cereal

5

6

7

8

9

10

6  **Look and write. Then read and number.**

| lunch | ~~breakfast~~ | dinner |

1

breakfast

2

3

a I like chicken and apples.

b I like toast and eggs.

c I like fish and vegetables. But I don't like rice.

7 Look and write.

cereal

grapes

fish

beans

There's some …

rice

_____

_____

_____

There are some …

_____

_____

_____

_____

burgers

rice

hot dogs

chicken

8 Look at Activity 7. Read and write the answers.

| Yes, there is.   No, there isn't.   Yes, there are.   No, there aren't. |

1 Is there any rice?   Yes, there is.

2 Is there any pizza? _____

3 Are there any bananas? _____

4 Are there any burgers? _____

9 **Read and tick (✓).**

		YES	NO
1	It is Princess Emily's birthday.	✓	
2	Princess Emily is happy.		
3	Princess Emily likes apples.		
4	Princess Emily doesn't like fish.		
5	Princess Emily likes pizza.		
6	Princess Emily doesn't like cake.		
7	Princess Emily likes Pippin.		

10 **Look and circle the healthy food and snacks.**

1

2

3

4

5

6

7

8

9

11 Read the words. Circle the pictures.

book   foot   look   moon

12 (2:58) **Listen and link the letters.**

ee   igh   e   oa

START   a   oo   o   FINISH

oo   ai   ai   oo

13 (2:59) **Listen and write the words.**

1 t oo   2 _____   3 _____   4 _____

14 (2:60) **Read aloud. Then listen and check.**

Look at the big moon. Look at the book, too.

15 Look and write.

mix	fry	cook	~~cut~~

1 cut

2 _____

3 _____

4 _____

16 Recipes. Read and write.

1

Hot fruit salad

a Cut some fruit.

b _____ the fruit in a pan.

c _____ the _____.

2

Pasta salad

a _____ some pasta.

b _____ some sweetcorn.

c Mix the _____ and _____.

3

Fish and chips

a _____ some _____.

b _____ some potatoes.

c _____ the potatoes.

Wider World

17 **Listen and circle.**

1 She likes (/ )

for (breakfast / lunch / dinner).

2 He likes ( /  / )

for (breakfast / lunch / dinner).

3 He likes (/  / )

for (breakfast / lunch / dinner).

18 **Complete. Then ask and write (✓) or (✗).**

	me	my friend
Do you like croissants for breakfast?		
Do you like pasta for lunch?		
Do you like fish and rice for dinner?		
Do you like _____?		
Do you like _____?		
Do you like _____?		

Unit Review

19 **Listen and circle. Then write.**

I like …
cereal
chicken
cheese
fish
apples
salad

I don't like …
toast
pizza
bread
bananas
eggs
rice

1 He _likes chicken_

and _____ .

2 He _____

or _____ .

20  **Read and circle. Then draw.**

This is my breakfast. There's some / any cereal and there's some / any toast.

There are some / any bananas and there's some / any juice.

There isn't some / any cheese and there aren't some / any apples.

I like breakfast!

About Me

21 **Read and write.**

~~some~~ any like don't fruit

This is my favourite dinner.

There's ¹ some pizza and there's some salad.

I ² _____ pizza and salad.

There aren't ³ _____ hot dogs. I ⁴ _____ like hot dogs.

And there's some fruit. I like ⁵ _____.

But I don't like bananas.

22  **Draw your favourite dinner. Then circle and write.**

This is my favourite dinner.

_____

_____

_____

_____

_____

_____

7 Clothes

1 **Find and write. Then colour.**

| dress | trousers | shoe | skirt | socks | ~~T-shirt~~ | hat | jacket |

1 an orange _T-shirt_

2 blue _____

3 a pink _____

4 a red _____

5 a brown _____

6 green _____

7 a purple _____

8 a black _____

2 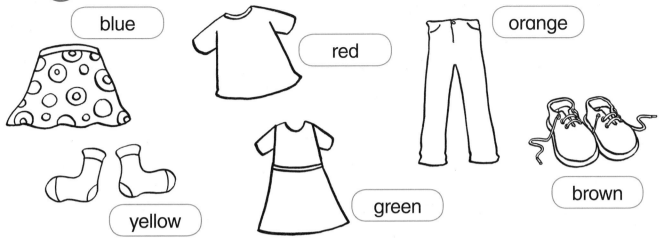 **Read and colour. Then read and write.**

1 I'm wearing _____brown_____ shoes and a _____ skirt.

2 I'm wearing a _____ T-shirt and _____ trousers.

3 I'm wearing a _____ dress and _____ socks.

3  **Look at Activity 2. Read and circle.**

1 Are you wearing brown shoes?   (Yes, I am.)/ No, I'm not.

2 Are you wearing a green T-shirt?   Yes, I am. / No, I'm not.

3 Are you wearing a yellow skirt?   Yes, I am. / No, I'm not.

4 Are you wearing a green dress?   Yes, I am. / No, I'm not.

4  **Read and answer about you.**

1 Are you wearing yellow socks? _____

2 Are you wearing a green T-shirt? _____

3 What are you wearing today? _____

_____

 **5** **Look and write.**

bed   boots   jumper   ~~pyjamas~~   pyjamas   school   shoes   T-shirt

1 Take off your pyjamas.

2 Put on your _____.

3 Put on your _____.

4 It's time for _____.

5 Take off your _____.

6 Take off your _____.

7 Put on your _____.

8 It's time for _____.

6 **Listen and match. Then colour.**

7 **Look, read and circle. Then colour.**

1

Would you like a red jumper?
Yes, I would. / No, I wouldn't.
I'd like a (red jumper / red shirt).

2

Would you like white trainers?
Yes, I would. / No, I wouldn't.
I'd like (a pink boot / pink boots).

3

Would you like a yellow jacket?
Yes, I would. / No, I wouldn't.
I'd like a (yellow shirt / yellow skirt).

4

Would you like blue pyjamas?
Yes, I would. / No, I wouldn't.
I'd like (a blue pyjamas / blue pyjamas).

Lesson 4 grammar (*What would you like?*)

8 **Read, look and match.**

1 I'm wearing brown shoes and a brown shirt.

2 I'm wearing a pink dress and one pink shoe!

3 I'm wearing blue trousers and orange shoes.

4 We're wearing hats. They're blue, black, and yellow.

9 **Look and write.**

| ~~Good morning.~~ Goodbye! Good night. I'm sorry. Please. Thank you. |

1
Good morning.

2

3

4

5

6

10   Read the words. Circle the pictures.

ar   ir   or   ur

car   girl   shark   surf

11 **Listen and link the letters.**

| ir | — | or | | ur | | r |

START

| o | | ck | | ir | | FINISH |

| ar | | ai | | ch | | ar |

12 **Listen and write the words.**

1 s ir _____   2 ___ ___ ___   3 ___ ___ ___   4 ___ ___ ___

13 **Read aloud. Then listen and check.**

See the girl surf. See the shark surf!

14 **Look and write.**

| chef | firefighter | ~~nurse~~ | police officer |

1

2

3

4

She's a
nurse_____.

He's a
_____.

He's a
_____.

She's a
_____.

15 **Read. Then look at Activity 14 and number.**

a I'm wearing a shirt, a black skirt and black shoes. I'm wearing a hat. I've got a badge on my hat. ☐

b I'm wearing a white dress, a hat and black shoes. ☐

c I'm wearing a coat and boots. I'm wearing a big helmet. ☐

d I'm wearing a T-shirt and trousers. I'm wearing white shoes and a tall hat. ☐

Wider World

16 **Colour and play.**

a

b

Are you wearing a yellow shirt?

Yes, I am.

No, I'm not.

17 **Look at Activity 16 and write.**

I'm wearing a _____ shirt and a _____ skirt. I'm wearing a _____ jacket. I'm wearing _____ boots. And I've got a _____ hat with flowers on it!

I'm wearing _____ trousers and a _____ jacket. I'm wearing _____ shoes. And I've got a _____ hat!

Unit Review

18 🔘 3:21 **Listen and tick (✓).**

1	purple dress	☐	pink dress	✓	pink skirt	☐
2	black trainers	☐	white trainers	☐	blue shoes	☐
3	purple skirt	☐	purple dress	☐	pink skirt	☐
4	brown shoes	☐	red socks	☐	red shoes	☐

19 ✏️ **Read and number. Then colour.**

1 I'm wearing yellow pyjamas.

2 I'm wearing red shoes.

3 I'm wearing black boots.

4 I'm wearing a purple jumper.

 a ☐

 b ☐

 c ┊

 d ☐

20 ✏️ **What are you wearing? Read and circle.**

1 Are you wearing pink pyjamas?   Yes, I am. / No, I'm not.

2 Are you wearing white socks?   Yes, I am. / No, I'm not.

3 Are you wearing black shoes?   Yes, I am. / No, I'm not.

4 Are you wearing glasses?   Yes, I am. / No, I'm not.

About Me

21 **Read and write. Then colour.**

| These | this | is | are | ~~wearing~~ | like |

I'm ¹ __wearing__ my favourite clothes.
² _____ are my favourite jeans and ³ _____ is my favourite T-shirt. My jeans ⁴ _____ blue and my T-shirt ⁵ _____ red. I'm not wearing black trainers. I'm wearing white trainers. I'd ⁶ _____ some black trainers. I'm wearing a green cap.

22  **Draw your favourite clothes. Then circle and write.**

I'm wearing my favourite clothes.

_____

_____

_____

_____

_____

8 Weather

 1 Look and write.

cloudy   rainy   snowy   stormy   ~~sunny~~   windy

What's the weather like?

It's ___sunny___.

What's the weather like?

It's _____.

What's the weather like?

It's _____.

What's the weather like?

It's _____.

What's the weather like?

It's _____.

What's the weather like?

It's _____.

2 3:29 **Listen and write. Then draw.**

rainy ~~snowy~~ sunny windy

1 He likes __snowy__ days.

2 She doesn't like _____ days.

3 She likes _____ days.

4 He doesn't like _____ days.

 3 **Read, write and circle.**

1 What's the weather like today?   It's _____.

2 Do you like sunny days?   Yes, I do. / No, I don't.

3 Do you like cloudy days?   Yes, I do. / No, I don't.

4 Do you like stormy days?   Yes, I do. / No, I don't.

Lesson 2 grammar (*What's the weather like? It's cloudy.*)

Look and write.

ride   take   fly   go   ~~make~~   read

1 make a snowman.

2 _____ for a walk.

3 _____ a bike.

4 _____ a photo.

5 _____ a kite.

6 _____ a book.

5 **Look, read and write.**

Monday	Tuesday	Wednesday	Thursday	Friday	Saturday

1 It's snowy. What day is it today?   It's Saturday .

2 It's windy. What day is it today?   It's _____.

3 It's rainy. What day is it today?   It's _____.

4 It's sunny. What day is it today?   It's _____.

5 It's stormy. What day is it today?   It's _____.

6 It's cloudy. What day is it today?   It's _____.

6 **Look and circle.**

1. That hat is (**mine** / yours)!

2. This hat is (mine / yours)!

3. Those boots are (mine / yours)!

4. And these boots are (mine / yours)!

7 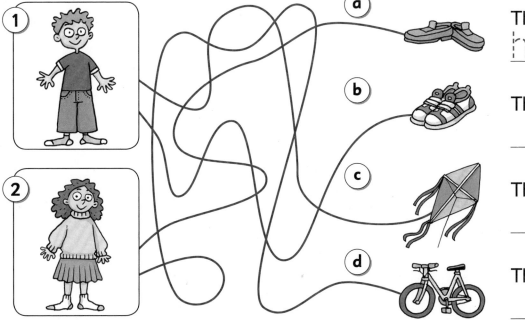 **Follow and write *his* or *hers*.**

a. These shoes are ~~hers~~ .

b. These trainers are _____ .

c. This kite is _____ .

d. This bike is _____ .

Lesson 4 grammar (*This/that (kite) is mine/yours/his/hers.*)

8 **Read and circle.**

STORY

1 What's the weather like?   It's stormy. / It's windy.

2 Is Princess Emily happy?   Yes, she is. / No, she isn't.

3 Does Princess Emily like Lindy's clothes?   Yes, she does. / No, she doesn't.

4 Does Pippin like Joe and Lindy?   Yes, he does. / No, he doesn't.

5 How many friends does Princess Emily have now?   One friend. / Three friends.

  9 **Look and tick (✓) the things you can share with other people.**

	friend(s)	sister(s)	brother(s)	parents

10 **Read the words. Circle the pictures.**

~~boy~~ cow cowboy down

11 (3:37) **Listen and link the letters.**

| ar | o | h | w |

START — | j | oy | oy | FINISH

| ow | y | p | ow |

12 (3:38) **Listen and write the words.**

1 ow   2 _____   3 _____   4 _____

13 (3:39) **Read aloud. Then listen and check.**

The boy watches the cowboy. The cow watches the boy.

14  **Look and write. Then listen and number.**

~~cold~~ freezing hot warm

a

_____

b

_____

c

_____

d

| 1 |

cold

15 **Read, look, and write (✓) or (✗).**

Sunday	Monday	Tuesday	Wednesday	Thursday	Friday	Saturday
☁	☀	🌀	🌧	🌨	☀	⛈

1 It's Tuesday. It's windy. ✓

2 It's Thursday. It's rainy.

3 It's Monday. Is it snowy?

4 It's Saturday. Is it stormy?

5 It's Sunday. It's cloudy.

6 It's Friday. It's sunny.

Wider World

16 **Listen and write.**

| January ~~August~~ September March July |

1
It's <u>August</u>.
It's sunny.

2
It's _____.
It's windy.

3
It's _____.
It's cloudy.

4
It's _____.
It's snowy.

5
It's _____.
It's rainy.

17 **What's the weather like in your country? Read and write.**

1 It's _____ in January.

2 It's _____ in March.

3 It's _____ in May.

4 It's _____ in August.

5 It's _____ in October.

6 It's _____ in December.

Unit Review

  Read, look and write A or B.

Picture A

Picture B

1 It's cloudy. **2** I'm wearing a T-shirt and trousers.

3 I've got a train. **4** I like pizza.

5 I'm wearing a dress. **6** I've got a doll.

7 I like chicken. **8** Look at my dog. It's big.

9 It's sunny. **10** I'm wearing boots.

About Me

19 **Read and write.**

| hat cold boots snowman doesn't ~~December~~ |

My favourite month is
¹December.
It's ² _____ and snowy
in my country. I'm wearing a
coat and big ³ _____.
This ⁴ _____ is
mine. He's got a ⁵ _____!
My cat ⁶ _____ like
the snow.

20  **Draw your favourite month and write.**

My favourite month is

_____.

_____

_____

_____

_____

Goodbye

1 Look and write.

duck   key   photo   ~~present~~   nuts   shoe
sunglasses   treasure chest   umbrella

1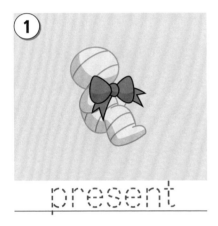

present

2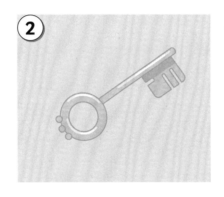

_____

3

_____

4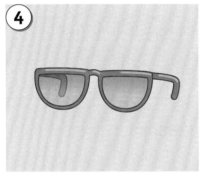

_____

5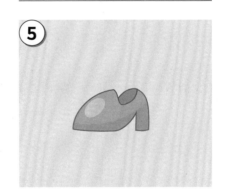

_____

6

_____

7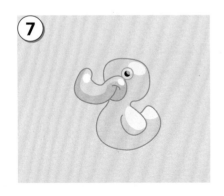

_____

8

_____

9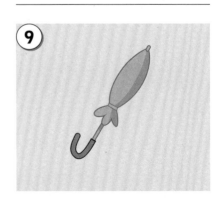

_____

Read and draw.

1 There's a photo on the TV.

2 There are some keys in the door.

3 There are some shoes under the sofa.

4 There's a duck in the box.

5 There are some sunglasses next to the lamp.

6 There's an umbrella behind the bag.

3 **Look at Activity 2. Read, circle and write.**

1 Where (is / (are)) the shoes?   It's / (They're) under the sofa.

2 Where (is / are) the duck?   It's / They're _____.

3 Where (is / are) the sunglasses?   It's / They're _____.

4 Where (is / are) the photo?   It's / They're _____.

4 **Listen and write (✓)or (✗). Then write.**

Sally					
has got	✗	✓			
would like	✗				

Sally has got a ___bike_____ and an _____.

She hasn't got a _____, a _____ or a _____.

She'd like a _____ and a _____. She wouldn't like a _____.

5 **Complete the chart for yourself. Then write.**

I've got					
I'd like					

I've got _____.

I haven't got _____.

I'd like _____.

I wouldn't like _____.

6 **Can you remember? Read and answer.**

1 What colour is Grandad's hair? _It's white._

2 Is Lindy's hair curly? _____

3 How many cousins has Lindy got? _____

4 What colour are Pippin's wings? _____

5 Has Princess Emily got a big nose? _____

6 Is Pippin Princess Emily's friend? _____

7 Does Grandad like fish? _____

8 Does Princess Emily like pizza? _____

a | Yes, he does.   **b** | It's ~~white~~.   **c** | Yes, he is.

d | No, she hasn't.   **e** | No, she doesn't.   **f** | Two.

g | No, it isn't. It's straight.   **h** | They're blue and red.

7 **Write three questions for your friend to answer.**

1 _____ ? _____.

2 _____ ? _____.

3 _____ ? _____.

Halloween

1 **Read and match.**

1 I'm a witch. I've got six sweets.

2 I'm a monster. I've got a pumpkin.

3 I'm a ghost. I've got four sweets.

4 I'm a pumpkin. I've got a bat.

a

b

c

d

e

f

g

h

2 **Read and circle.**

1 Do you like sweets?   Yes, I do. / No, I don't.

2 Do you like bats?   Yes, I do. / No, I don't.

3 Do you like pumpkins?   Yes, I do. / No, I don't.

4 Do you like Halloween?   Yes, I do. / No, I don't.

Christmas

1 **Look and write.**

present ~~Santa~~ sack star stocking card Christmas tree

1 Santa **2** _____ **3** _____ **4** _____

5 _____ **6** _____ **7** _____

2 **Look and colour.**

1 = red   **2** = green   **3** = black   **4** = blue   **5** = yellow

Easter

1 Read and match.

1 Wake up, Easter Bunny!

2 Jump, Easter Bunny!

3 Turn around, Easter Bunny!

4 Fall down, Easter Bunny!

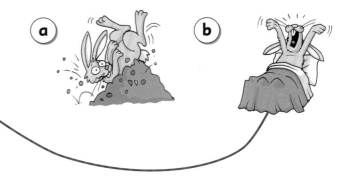

2 Count and write.

1 How many chicks? 5

2 How many flowers?

3 How many eggs?

4 How many rabbits?

Summer fun

1 Look and write.

sand   sea   sandcastle   bucket   ~~spade~~   shell

1 _spade_

2 _____
3 _____
4 _____
5 _____
6 _____

2 Sand art! Join the dots and write.

1

2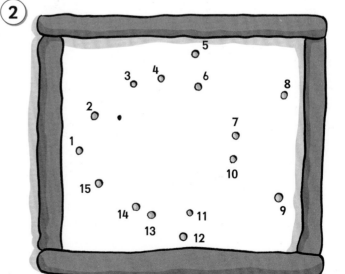

It's a _____.   It's a _____.

1 Review

1 Write the questions. Then say.

1 (name?) (your) (What's)   What's your name?

2 (are) (How) (you?)   _____

3 (your) (birthday?) (When's)   _____

4 (today?) (day) (What) (it) (is)   _____

2 Read and circle. Then write.

1   What's (this)/ that ?
     (It's)/ They're a teddy bear .

2   What are these / those ?
     It's / They're _____.

3   What's this / that ?
     It's / They're a _____.

4   What are these / those ?
     It's / They're _____.

How many cars are there? There are _____ cars.

How many boats are there? _____.

1 Read and circle.

1 (There's / **There are**) two chairs.
2 (There's / There are) a sofa.
3 There's a teddy (on / under) the sofa.
4 (There's / There are) a table.
5 There's a doll (behind / next to) the TV.
6 There's a ball (in / on) a chair.

2 Read and circle.

Who's (**he** / she?)   (**He's** / She's) my uncle.

Who are (they / there?)   (They're / There) my cousins.

Where's my aunt?   (He's / She's) (on / under) the sofa.

3

1 **Choose and write.**

| Touch | can't | can | ~~Wave~~ | you | Point |

_____Wave_____ your arms.

_____ your fingers.

_____ your toes.

Oh, no!
I _____
touch my toes.

Can _____
touch your toes?

Yes, I _____.

1 **Read and draw.**

I haven't got small eyes. I've got big eyes.

I've got a small nose and a small mouth.

I've got big ears. My hair is long and curly.

2 **Write *Yes, she has.* or *No, she hasn't.***

1 Has she got short hair? No, she hasn't.

2 Has she got curly hair? _____

3 Has she got small eyes? _____

4 Has she got a small mouth? _____

3 **Write correct sentences.**

1 She's got a big nose. She hasn't got a big nose. She's got a small nose.

2 She's got straight hair. _____

_____

3 She's got small ears. _____

_____

5

1 **Circle and write.**

It isn't (big / small). It's (big / small).
(It's / They're) black.
It's got _____ legs.
(It's / They're) a _____.

(It's / They're) small.
They aren't (black / white). They're
(black / white).
They've got _____ legs.
(It's / They're) _____.

2  **Look at Activity 1. Read and match.**

1 Are the ducks brown?

2 Is the horse big?

3 Are the ducks small?

4 Is the horse grey?

a Yes, it is.

b No, it isn't.

c No, they aren't.

d Yes, they are.

6

1 **Read and circle.**

	✓	✓	✗	✓	✗	✗
	✗	✓	✓	✗	✓	✓

1 He (likes / doesn't) like fish.

2 She (likes / doesn't) like apples.

3 Does he like bananas? (Yes, he does. / No, he doesn't).

4 Does she like chicken? (Yes, she does. / No, she doesn't).

2 **Read and circle. Then draw.**

There's (some / any) cheese.

There isn't (some / any) milk.

There are (some / any) apples.

There aren't (some / any) bananas.

3 **Look at Activity 2. Read and match.**

1 Is there any cheese?   **a** No, there aren't.

2 Is there any pizza?   **b** Yes, there is.

3 Are there any apples?   **c** Yes, there are.

4 Are there any beans?   **d** No, there isn't.

7

1 **Choose and write.**

I'm   purple   not   am   ~~wearing~~   would   Are   like

Are you ___wearing___ shoes and socks?

Yes, I _____.

_____ wearing blue shoes and pink socks.

No, I'm _____.

_____ you wearing purple shoes?

Would you _____ some purple shoes?

Yes, I _____. Thank you!

Now I'm wearing _____ shoes and pink socks!

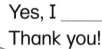

1 **Choose and write.**

| mine | They're | windy | that | do | those | ~~weather~~ | like |

What's the
weather like?

It's _____.
Good!

Do you _____
windy days?

Yes, I _____.

What are
_____?

_____ kites.

This kite is _____
and _____ kite
is yours.

I like windy days!

Picture dictionary

Unit 1

 My toys

| train | bike | ball | car | doll | boat | teddy bear | kite |

 Numbers

| 10 ten | 11 eleven | 12 twelve | 13 thirteen | 14 fourteen | 15 fifteen |

| 16 sixteen | 17 seventeen | 18 eighteen | 19 nineteen | 20 twenty | 21 twenty-one |

| 22 twenty-two | 23 twenty-three | 24 twenty-four | 25 twenty-five | 26 twenty-six | 27 twenty-seven |

| 28 twenty-eight | 29 twenty-nine | 30 thirty | 40 forty | 50 fifty |

 CLIL: Social Science

| bus | motorbike | lorry | plane | helicopter | boat | car | train |

Unit 2

 My family (1)

daughter   son

aunt   uncle

granny   grandad

cousins

 My house

house

flat

hall

kitchen

living room

bedroom

bathroom

attic

 CLIL: My family (2)

baby

young

children

parents

grandparents

old

My body (1)

shake your body

nod your head

wave your arms

point your fingers

touch your toes

clap your hands

stamp your feet

move your legs

 My body (2)

swim

climb

catch a ball

stand on your head

throw a ball

swing

do cartwheels

do the splits

 CLIL: P.E.

pull

push

kick

skip

Unit 4

 My face

hair

ears

eyes

nose

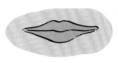

mouth

 My hair

long

short

curly

straight

dark

blond

neat

messy

 CLIL: Maths

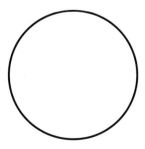

circle

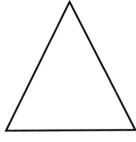

triangle

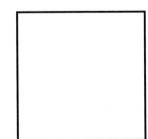

square

rectangle

Unit 5

 ## Animals (1)

duck

sheep

goat

horse

hen

cow

turkey

 ## Animals (2)

bat

crow

frog

skunk

owl

lizard

rat

fox

 ## CLIL: Science

ostrich

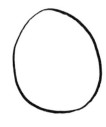
ostrich egg

ostrich nest

ostrich chick

Unit 6

 Food (1)

rice

bananas

pizza

burger

fish

chicken

apples

hot dogs

eggs

 Food (2)

cereal

grapes

potatoes

pancakes

beans

pineapple

coconut

pasta

sweetcorn

toast

 CLIL: Food science

cut

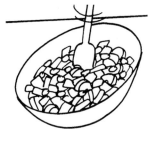
mix

fry

cook

Unit 7

 ## Clothes (1)

dress

T-shirt

socks

skirt

shoes

trousers

jacket

hat

 ## Clothes (2)

pyjamas

trainers

a shirt

a coat

jeans

a helmet

a cap

a jumper

glasses

boots

a badge

 ## CLIL: Social science

nurse

police officer

firefighter

chef

Unit 8

 ## Weather

windy   rainy   sunny   snowy   cloudy   stormy

 ## Activities

ride a bike   fly a kite   make a snowman   go for a walk

go to the beach   read a book   take a photo   watch TV

 ## CLIL: Social science

freezing   cold   warm   hot

Pearson Education Limited
Edinburgh Gate
Harlow
Essex CM20 2JE
England
and Associated Companies throughout the world.

www.islands.pearson.com

First published 2012
Ninth impression 2019
ISBN: 978-1-4082-9007-1

Set in Fiendstar 17/21pt
Printed in Slovakia by Neografia

Picture Credits
The Publisher would like to thank the following for their kind permission to reproduce their photographs:

(Key: b-bottom; c-centre; l-left; r-right; t-top)

Alamy Images: MIXA 106 (skipping); **DK Images:** 109 (chicken); **Fotolia.com:** Sébastien Garcia 104 (teddy bear), Irina Khomenko 108 (turkey), Sergey Peterman 109 (burger), Studio M 109 (hot dogs); **iStockphoto:** DNY59 109 (bananas), garysludden 110 (shoes), Clayton Hansen 110 (t-shirt), Eric Isselée 108 (chicken), 108 (horse), 108 (sheep), Ju-Lee 108 (duck), MistikaS 109 (apples), Pelham Mitchinson 109 (eggs), Sabina Schaaf 109 (salad), Gina Smith 110 (trousers); **Pearson Education Ltd:** Trevor Clifford 106 (arms up), 106 (clapping), 106 (girl bending), 106 (nodding), Studio 8 106 (move legs); **Photolibrary. com:** Mike Kenip 106 (my body); **Shutterstock.com:** 110 (dress), arkashal905 109 (pizza), bat-2 104 (doll), Gemenacom 104 (bicycle), Iwona Grodzka 104 (kite), Rafa Irusta 110 (socks), Karkas 110 (jacket), 110 (skirt), katja kodba 108 (cow), Carlos Moura 104 (train), Neirfy 109 (fish), Oculo 104 (car), Nikolai Pozdeev 109 (rice), SergiyN 106 (point), TerraceStudio 110 (hat); **Thinkstock:** Hemera 108 (goat), PhotoObjects.net 104 (ball), 104 (boat)

All other images © Pearson Education

Every effort has been made to trace the copyright holders and we apologise in advance for any unintentional omissions. We would be pleased to insert the appropriate acknowledgement in any subsequent edition of this publication.

Illustration Acknowledgements
Moreno Chiacchiera (Beehive Illustration), HL Studios, Sue King (Plum Pudding Illustration).